Words From Above

Published by BooxAi
ISBN: 978-965-578-196-0

Words From Above

Inspired

Dr. Daniel Simon Pierre

Preface

This book is about all my original thoughts, my personal, and private relationships with almighty God.

I became a Christian at the age of 15 when I got baptized in a trinitarian fashion. I am blessed to have been born and raised in a Christian family of both parents.

Nonetheless, my walk with God and Jesus Christ compelled me to get rebaptized in the name of Jesus Christ for the remission of my sins (Acts 2:38). I did not always live for Christ or was part of the church, but God reluctantly sought me out because of his love. As a backslider, I had no choice but to come home, just like the prodigal son did.

I thank my wife for being my partner in Christ for 23 years, and for propelling me to write from my heart. I think that my poems and writing have matured through the years.

I think and know that the readers will be in touch religiously, have a relationship with Christ, and be compelled to write their inner thoughts and feelings. My advice to the reader is to open your heart, try God, accept the Lord Jesus as your Lord and personal savior, walk with him, and try to live a holy life. Yes, also remember to attend church regularly, go to a Bible study class, or Sunday school, volunteer at a homeless shelter, and find your inner peace.

My intention is simply to keep it real, to touch every dormant religious nerve, and to have the reader think of God and eternity.

Lastly, I desire to connect to each of my readers on a religious basis, and I wish for them to be safe, and see them all in heaven one day.

God loves you and bless you.

Who I am?

To be or not to be that is the question.
To question or not to question that is to be.

What is to be?
What shall be the question?
What shall it be?
What shall be asked?
What shall it be?
What shall be answered?

Perhaps, nothing.
Perhaps, something.
Perhaps, no one.
Must be someone.

Who shall it be?
Who will find out?

Maybe you.
Maybe me.
You may see.

Who it shall be?

God

Who is God, who is He, who is She, who is it?
What is God, what is He, what is She, what is it?
When is God, when is He, when is She, when should it come?
Where is God, where is He, where is She, where would it be?
Why is God, why is He, why is She, why is it not to me?
How is God, how is He, how is She, and how it feels?

Love

Love is abstract, love is concret.
Love is fogy, sometimes solid.

Solid and painful when I feel hurt,
whenever and each time you hurt my heart with pain.

Hurting so deeply that is felt in my marrow,
the deepest part of me where I grow.

Growing each day with undetermined length,
that is how long my love will stand.

My Alphabet

A is for apple
B is for boy
C is for cat
D is for dog
E is for elephant
F is for fun
G is for good
H is for hot
I is for imagine
K is kitty
L is for love
M is for mom
N is for not
O is for open
P is for purple
Q is for question
R is for respect
S is for sex
T is for top
U is for utilize
V is for victory
W is for water
X is for Xerox
Y is for yellow
Z is for zoo

Covetousness

Give me more, give me now.
Give me more, and give it to me now.

Give me more than I can keep.
Go ahead, I have room for it all.

Give me more than I can pay
for there is always a layaway.

Give it to me, make it fit, and make it feel good.
I want it, I like it, go ahead give it to me now.

Olympiad

Athens, god Apollo, son Hercules
Brazil, braziers, capital of breast augmentations
Chicago, passing-smelling winds, presidential corruption
Atlanta, sad bumming, false accusation
Greece, swim like a fish, record eight gold medals
Montreal, clean and cold, the bill paid in 2009
Los Angeles, the Crips and the Bloods,
sexy blond babes and the beach boys.
Moscow, cold war, did not go through this boycott.
Madrid, good food, salsa music, and merengue.
Mexico City, siesta, don't drink the water,
and do not breathe polluted air.

Hurricanes

Sucks now only for a time
dynasty as an independent
5 NCAA football championships,
Big East in your face, ass whooping with consistency
ACC same ass-kicking for all
Swagger, boasting, showboating
53 home games winning streaks
Many Heisman's winners
Most drafted players in the NFL,
wide right, right left in your face.
This is the "U" that I remember.

Death

Oh death, where is thy sting?
Oh death, where is thy victory?

Laugh now, but death cries later.

Oh death where is thy sting?
Oh death, where is thy victory?

Your sting may hurt me now,
but joy comes in the morning.

Oh death where is thy sting?
Oh death where is thy victory?

Victor, but not the victim no more.
Victory is mine in the name of Jesus.

The Father

I'm the Father
Lord of all, and Lord for all
Father of all mankind, Father on your mind

My God, the God, your God, the only true God.
Most high, not low, but high above all and surely above the clouds.
The everlasting God.

The Lord-will-provide
The Lord
The Lord God of heaven
Lord God
Beer Lahai Roi

What His Name

Savior
Lamb of God
Redeemer
Messiah
Jesus
Jesus Christ
Jesus the Christ
Bright of the morning star
Bread of life
Resurrection and life
Lion of the Tribe of Judah
Holly one
Alpha and Omega
The way, the truth, and the life
Immanuel
God with us
The child
A Nazarene
Lord
The Lord
Son of God
Lord our Lords
King of Kings
Teacher
Master
Son of man
Son of David
Son
John the Baptizer
Elijah, Jeremiah, the prophet

Son of the living God
Rabbi
I'm the God of Abraham, the God of Isaac, and the God of Jacob
Jesus of Nazareth
King of the Jews
Son of the highest God
Carpenter
The son of Marie and brother of Joseph, James, Judas, and Simon
Beloved son
Abba
Father
Son of the highest
Son of Joseph
Master of the Sabbath

Holly Spirit

Comforter
Holly Ghost
Holly Spirit
The one to come
God
Third person of the trinity
Fire
Wind

Golf

Pot, three iron
Hole in one
Beardy that does not fly
Boggy bad play
Par and ego
Subpart like a submarine
Even par, even Steven
Ruff not smooth
Lake floating
Sinker in the sand

Tennis

Net and rackets
John McEnroe arguing calls and smashing his rockets
Ace
Jimmy Connors professionalism and class on the court
Deuce
Arthur Ashe first African-American grand slam winner
Breakpoint
Even Lindle European champ
Match point
Billy Jean King made history by beating a man
Fault
Chris Everett's sweetness and elegance in action
Judge
Martina Navratilova like the supernova
Line judge
The Williams's sister's pure brute force and big muscles
White lines and six ball boys.

Hockey

Wayne Gretzky the great French one,
Youngest rewrites record book, made history early.

Guy Lafleur french talented,
Skate like a swan with no helmet.

Gordy Orr is legendary,
A vanguard, trailblazer, historic.

Grand Fur, the black rubber pock doesn't pass him,
Guard the net like Fort Knox.

Ken Dryden protects the Madison Square Garden,
Another save, one more stop, another victory

Eric Lindros powerfully, but short leaves career,
city of love, love to skate, and hit hard against the glass.

Mario Lemieux, French also, wears a helmet.
Stuck around, sickness retired too prematurely.

Sex

What is this immense feeling
that is irresistible and indescribable?
Orgasm to the max, stimulating all my senses,
and quite unbelievable

Climatic moment,
hot erotic passion.
Seconds at most,
but long-lasting hot memories and emotions.

More mental than physical, you know.
Man thinks of me every six seconds they say.

Women don't get enough of me I know.
But I can also be obtained for a small fee that is.

Football

Summer, humid, hot, drops of sweats
Winter, cold, freezing, blizzards
Raining, muddy, sleeper
Helmets, clits, and pads
Stadium, coliseum, white lines, man in black stripes
Captains at midfield, shake hands, coin toss, head or tail
Whistle blows, kick-off, and game on the way
Punting team, receiving team, and special team
First down, second down, third down, and fourth down
Yardage, move the oval leather pig skin
Offense and defense adjust, couple of sacks,
fourth down, punt again
Another team, punt return, good blockage,
crosses the goal line
Touch down, six points, one extra point,
the crowd goes wild.

Basketball

Bill Russell, 11 rings, old great timer
Wilt Chamberlain, once scored 100 points,
dominating the paint
Julius Irving, "Doctor J", dunks from the top
Kareem Abdul Jabbar, skyhook unstoppable
Larry Bird, unpassable shooting
Irving "Magic" Johnson, no look pass, played all positions
Dominic Wilkins, dunking champion and MVP
Darrel Dunken, pure power, broke baskets many times
Shaquille "Shaq" O'Neal, broke basket too,
rapper and comedian.
Kobe Bryan, once scored 81, gone too soon.
Dewayne Wade, unstoppable in the paint.
LeBron "King "James, the best player in the NBA,
but not a champion yet.
Michael "Air "Jordan, 3 dunking titles,
6 times finals MVP, 6 championships,
9 scoring titles, 2 Olympic gold medals,
4 times league MVP, no look free throw,
spectacular moves by Michael Jordan, exclaimed Marv Albert.

Baseball

Empire
First base Empire
Second base Empire
Third base Empire

First base
Second base
Third base
Home plate

Single play
Double play
Triple pay

Single
Double
Triple
Home run

Strike one
Stick two
Stick three
You're out

Ball one
Ball two
Ball three
Walked

One run
Two runs
Three runs
Grand slam

God Two

God is the one that created you,
according to his image, according to his likeness.

God is good all the time, and all the time God is surely good,
even though you may not understand his purpose for you.

Things may even never seem to go your way,
God is still all-knowing, all-seeing, and all-powerful

God is infinite and everlasting,
although you can't begin to comprehend its beginning or end.

God is the one that makes the earth rotate around the sun,
and provide its warmth while growing its vegetation.

God makes the stars and moon fit harmoniously in the firmament,
that provides illumination after the sun says goodnight.

God is God all by himself and does not need anyone's help,
does not need to be defined, explained, boxed in, and scientifically
theorized.

Jesus

Jesus is the answer to the world today,
in a world full of confusion, turmoil, wars, and rumors of wars,
I need Jesus.

Oh, how I love Jesus.
How can you love him and not your neighbor?
You need Jesus.

Jesus is the way, the truth, and the life.
We must show the way, tell the truth, and save lives.
We need Jesus.

Holly Ghost

Holly Ghost comes into this place
Feels me and makes me whole
As whole as I can be
To continue my journey
On this earth, in this world

Food

Cold food
Hot food
Spicy food

Liquid food
Solid food
Junk food

Palatable
Tasty
Nasty

American
Canadian
European

Taste bugs
Delicious
Gordon blue

Family

Abraham, Isaac, and Jacob
Nucleus, extended and blended
Mother, father, children
Diapers, bottles, and wipers
Fights, fits, and near miss
Love you, hate you, and can't do without you
Calls 911, runs away, and DCF
Need you, don't care, won't swear

Here I am

Here I am Lord, use me
Make me, shape me, and mold me
Send me and I will go
Charge me and I will grow
Grow to show the world
How much you love them
That you sent your only son
To die for me in my place
A place of desolation, agony, shame
For indeed you remember my name
Long ago written in the Lamb Book of life
With your indelible blood that was shed on the cross
Open is the first book then the second book
Whose names not found written
Will not enter the promised land.

Politics

Politics is a dirty game,
if you don't have the stomach for it, don't play the game.

Republicans, Democrats, Independents.

Politics is hot and steamy,
if you can't stand the heat, get out of the kitchen.

Conservatives, Liberals, undecided.

Politic is nasty,
if you want to stay clean, don't take illegal kickbacks.

Right, left, and center.

Executive branch,
white house, Oval Office, 1600 Pennsylvania Avenue,
"I did not have sex with that woman", community organizer,
or Illinois junior senator, just speeches, just words.

Acorn, register, vote often.

Legislative Branch,
bills, the president signed or vetoed, and laws passed.

Majority, sixty percent, philoboster.

Judicial Branch,
district court, circuit court, appellate court, Supreme Court.

Liberal, conservative, constitutional judges.

Senators,
town meetings, poles, votes to benefit constituents; do for me first,
awesome,
well-spoken, good speeches.

Do as I say, immorality, caught with pants down.

Congressmen,
enact laws for others to follow but not for them.
Don't watch me, follow the law, don't you get it?

Vice president,
presides over the House, tie bracer, in the shadow,
wish he was the president.

Councilmen, commissioners, mayors,
small timers, insignificant.

Governors,
most to become presidents, term limit,
and Watergate.

Chapter 8

S ilence reigned for a moment. The quilts looked down on them. "Angie's younger sister. That's your grandmother, Dana?" Margo was the first to speak.

"Yes, it must be so," Dana answered quietly.

"Your grandmother lost her sister and then her parents, too, in a short time, less than a year, it sounds like." Alice's summary was heartfelt and accurate.

"I never knew," Edna said so quietly that she sounded far away.

"Poor Angie. She was so alone. If we had known...." Janet couldn't finish what they were all feeling.

"I think you ladies became her family," Dana replied simply and warmly.

"But she never told us," Margo's regret was answered by Edna's assurance, "No, she must have had her reasons."

"I bet he was handsome," Alice said, braving a wistful smile.

Everyone stared at her. "Who was handsome?" Edna fairly demanded.

"Well, you know, George. The intern? Er, 'Physicians' Assistant,' that's what Angie called him, right?" Alice looked from one to another.

"You're such a romantic, Alice," Janet chided her friend.

"The next postmark is August 1966," Dana held up the letter.

The group huddled closer—except for Edna, who grew stern and held back tears for her friend's secret tragedies.

Dana's voice was softer as she read the following letter.

RONNI CHAVEZ

August 22, 1966

Worcester State Hospital

Stinson Ward

Dear Sis,

I want you to know I was only helping. Matron is writing to you about "my incident," George said he would mail this, so I hope you will hear my side first.

We are always short of bed linens and blankets here—short of everything, as it happens. Let me start over. See, the men patients work on the farm to grow our food. I work in the canning kitchen. Matron says that will show the Community Center social workers that I can get a job and take care of you.

I had a plan to help make more blankets. My new room is dreary, and my new roommates are even drearier. I wanted to make something beautiful, like the hexagon tiles in my old room. And make a fun project too.

I puzzled them together on the ballroom floor, including my roommates. My plan would help the whole ward, and if it worked, the entire hospital could do it, too. That would show the social workers I am ready to go home to you.

So, I got scissors from the stationary desk in the hospital library. I know that wasn't allowed, but I needed to prove my plan. My new roommate, Mary, works in the laundry. Sometimes, she comes back with needles or pins stuck in the hem of her dress. She holds them there when she is working, then forgets about them. So, I have collected a few. My plan came together when she left a spool of thread in her pocket. I told Mary I would return it to Matron for her, but I kept it. I'm telling you everything, Sis, so you'll know I'm not crazy.

The only thing left to do was cut some fabric. I cut the curtains in our room, plus some aprons from the kitchen. I cut small squares and thin rectangles. I worked at night while my roommates were asleep. I wasn't tired, not for days. Sis, it looked great! When the curtains were opened during the day, you wouldn't even notice the missing patches. But when they were shut, glorious! The moonlight mended the holes and dappled the whole room. I wish you could have seen it.

When I sorted all the pieces, I puzzled them together on the floor of the ballroom where we have movie nights. Mary and I started sewing the patches together. Anyone who came into the ballroom could help if they promised to keep it a secret until we finished the new blankets. You know, it was the most fun they had all year. My new roommate, Penny, even said she was glad to see me happy for a change.

Then, last night, an Attendant came to set up the movie projector. And he told Matron about my blanket project. Matron agreed we need blankets, but she said we need curtains too. Still, I think she liked my idea. She collected the parts we had finished. I saw her hide them in a cupboard when the Doctor was called. Then Doctor S. said I have "inappropriate behavior," and "lack ability to function normally," plus even more dumb complaints, and he plans to increase my medications.

I don't know if I will get to write to you again. Please remember your big sister and that I love you.

Always, Angie

Now, Edna was smiling. "That's my girl!" she punched the air with a fist. "That's the Angie I know—I knew."

"So, Angie started trying to teach herself quilting- in an asylum...when they needed blankets," Janet troubled over the circumstances. "No wonder she was such a good teacher."

"I thought we were making quilts for fun," said Margo. "I never knew it meant so much to Angie."

"But how did she get here," Janet was still reconciling.

Edna put her arm around Janet. "It was a long time ago. She must have been very young in these letters. Only 20, or 21?"

"Nearly sixty years," about the same time Margo herself was born.

"Can you continue, Dana? We can leave anytime you wish," Alice's encouragement was sincere.

"Just say when," even Janet nodded in support.

Professor Stanly watched the quilts overhead, listening quietly.

"One last chance for answers," said Dana, brushing off possible protestations and opening the final letter. "Postmark, October. Getting to the end of the year."

But this letter was different from the others.

Chapter 9

"What is this? It's not, Aunt Angie." Dana's voice had an edge; the cascading revelations were overtaking her patience.

"Let me see. How do you read this? "Margo tried to puzzle the letter.

"Look at the letterhead. It's from the Matron." Alice always read the complete pattern first.

"Let me see," Edna took the letter. Then Edna smirked. Then she giggled. She passed the letter to Janet, who turned it around a few times until she, too, began to laugh.

"What's so funny," Alice took the letter. "Ohhhh....quilting is addictive!"

Margo peered over Dana's shoulder. "Yes, Matron has caught the bug, too!"

There were glad tears between the friends and too much laughter for Dana to understand.

"You all must be crazy," Dana began to shake her head.

"Look at the letter from back here," Margo held it out at arms' length. "What do you see."

"I see...I think I see....is that a quilt?" Dana's eyes must be too tired. When is a letter a quilt?

"A log cabin block," confided Edna with pride.

"That is the quilt Angie was trying to make with the curtains!" Janet couldn't contain her glee at the reveal. "See, thin rectangles with a center square."

"Look," Alice pointed, "You start with the square in the center, then you keep turning right, adding longer and longer rectangles. Here, then here...see?"

"I think..yes!" Dana found herself laughing, too. Beginning in the tiny center square, Dana read the Matron's cramped writing. She turned the letter right, reading a short rectangle. Then she turned the letter upside down to read the next. As she found the piecing order, Dana read the good news faster, turning the letter in circles as she went.

October 2, 1966

Worcester State Hospital

Office of The Matron

To: Mr. & Mrs. Taylor,

I am sending news of our patient Angela Lyons, for her younger sister, your ward. During the storm this week, our facility lost all electrical power. Normally, this is not cause for alarm as it is an old building, approaching a centennial anniversary, in fact. However, Angela gained advantage of the circumstances and was able to escape the hospital.

I wish your newly formed family peace for the coming holidays and in the New Year. Goodness knows we could all benefit from pleasant and peaceful times in 1967.

Best of Luck,

Matron Sullivan

THE CRAZY QUILTER

Best of Luck,
Matron Sullivan

I wish your newly formed family peace

Normally, this is not
cause for concern,

I am sending news
of our patient,

ANGELA LYONS,

October 2, 1966
Worcester
State
Hospital
Office of
The Matron

To Mr. &
Mrs. Taylor,

During the storm this
week, our facility lost
all electrical power.

the

was able to escape

and
hospital during the storm.

as it is an old building,
approaching a centennial, in fact.

for the coming holidays and the New Year.

for her younger sister,
your ward.

However, Angela gained advantage
of the circumstances,

Goodness knows, we could all benefit from pleasant
and peaceful times in 1967.

• • • •

ANGIE ESCAPED FROM the hospital! And her first quilting project, alive - at least in spirit. Dana's heart zoomed at the news of Aunt Angie's escape.

"Angie, she made it," Janet was visibly relieved. Margo hugged her. Still laughing between tears, Alice dried her eyes and bounced on her heels as close to jumping for joy as an old lady could be.

The quilters were bursting with joy for their friend's salvation and the magical remedy she had found. Only Professor Stanley sat still on the bar stool, looking out the window at the eventide.

That sight stopped Dana. Like an arrow falling from the sky, clarity struck Dana from her mind through her heart. "Professor, Stanley," she called out. "Is your given name George?"

Chapter 10

"I helped Angie escape. Although, I hadn't planned it," Professor Stanley admitted with his head held high, and no one interrupted George's story.

"After the 'blanket incident,' as we termed it in the staff room, I was impressed how Angela had discovered her own therapy through geometry. Putting shapes together with stitches. It was art, and it was useful. An ideal recipe for treatment. Most importantly, she wished to involve her fellow inmates—to work with others. Angie wanted them to find joy in the work and share in the purpose she had found. This was significant progress from her previous melancholy and anhedonia."

Professor Stanley paused, amazed even now after so many years.

"Initially, I argued with my superiors. They saw Angie's blanket project as a manic and chaotic episode. Cutting up the curtains was considered an attack on the Institution. That she organized getting scissors, needles, and thread; this only deemed her dangerous."

"The enhanced drugs they prescribed left her catatonic. She barely knew where she was—dragging her feet when anyone managed to get her to move. Sitting all day in the sun-room, not even looking out the window. She wasn't allowed in the library anymore. And her old paranoia was returning. So, when the power went out during the storm, it was at the end of my shift, but I went back to check on her anyway."

The ladies listened silently, riveted by the discovery that there were, in fact, two old friends they hadn't known.

"My concerns were correct; Angie was already anxious because of the storm. In fact, she thought I was there to take her to electroshock. She wailed and tried to hide in the wardrobe closet of their room. This, in turn, was upsetting her roommates."

He shook his head, recalling the despair of a young intern.

"It was all escalating needlessly. I would have to call the security attendants if I couldn't soon get control of the patients."

"So I sat on the floor next to the closet. I talked to Angie through the door. I told her about the quilt I had on my bed when I was young. It was red and gray, and my brother's bed had a matching quilt, except his quilt was blue. They had saw-tooth fringe around the edges and tied with yarn knots. Between flashes of lightning, she opened the closet door a crack. I passed her my handkerchief, and she dried her eyes. I asked her, 'Miss Lyons, will you trust me?' And she nodded and put out her hand for me to help her from the closet."

George smiled wistfully, seeing his younger self, a student doctor breaking out a patient. Who was the crazy one?

"Well, I never let go. I just walked with Angie, holding her hand, straight down the halls. Then I gave her my lab coat to wear as we crossed the big sun-room. In the dark asylum, she appeared exactly as Doctor Lynn, the only female clinician. We crossed through the sun-room and out the back door to my car. The hospital was dark; staff were all gone from their offices, checking on patients. We were just lucky that we never ran into anyone."

The professor shrugged.

"I wasn't scared until we were in the car. Suddenly, I was out of ideas. 'Where do you want to go?' I asked Angie. 'Take me to my sister,' was all she said. We couldn't drive around in the storm, so I parked at a nearby church, hoping we wouldn't look too out of place. Sitting in the car amid the storm, we made a plan."

"First, get new clothes, then evaluate a treatment without medications. I knew the authorities would check all the staff homes to rule out inside help, so we stayed at a hotel for two nights. After that, I told my landlord that my sister was visiting, and Angie moved to my apartment for a month until I could afford a nearby room for her."

"I found that odd orange and black quilt and the music box at an antique store. They were to keep her engaged while I was at work. She mended the quilt and spent days redrawing the blocks on paper and coloring them in again and again with crayons. She changed the colors each time, adding different quilting designs. The patterns looked better and better. The music box likewise served as a reliable repetition for engagement. Soon, she got a volunteer job at the library in Shrewsberry and then a quilting class, and you can see the rest."

He gestured around to the quilts on the walls. Each one witnesses to the tale, hovering like guardian angels above the little group.

"At first, I returned to the hospital to avoid suspicion. I want to say we had an exciting escape with flying bedpans or something more heroic. But it was thanks to our simple evasion that I managed to keep up appearances and avoid a statewide manhunt."

"To begin with, I bribed Mary with a box of chocolates. Suddenly, none of Angie's roommates even remembered the storm, if Angie had said anything, or how she had left. Next, I requested an emergency bereavement break from school and the hospital internship. Can you believe that the administration never even asked me for paperwork? The last thing I did was to take these three letters from the Matron's office files."

"All the letters, as you see, were returned to the sender, so we didn't know where your grandmother was, Dana. We visited the address, of course. That was a sad day. Angie started a log cabin quilt. She was a terror, ripping up fabrics I bought at TG&Y. And most of my ties went missing at that time."

"Now and then, we would try again to find her sister's name in the phone book. We considered using a private detective but decided that would bring too much attention. When the internet became a viable tool for locating people, we only found your grandmother's obituary. Angie began a compass quilt that day. Yes, same as that music box. But it was through that obituary that we found your name, Dana, to have you included in Angie's will."

"Eventually, I was able to finish school, but I couldn't be a clinician again. Too many unethical secrets. Although, no one looked too hard to find Angie. They figured she would get into trouble and be brought back, that she couldn't exist without their care. You must understand that it wasn't a bad place. The staff were good, for the times. She just didn't belong there."

The ladies nodded their understanding: Dana, plus Angie's old friends.

"Angie was my patient. I had to stay with her. I had to make sure she caused no harm to herself or to anyone else. There were a few more hard days over the years. But she was fine as long as she kept quilting. I figured the best way to keep that going was to help set up this shop here."

The Professor, Angie's oldest friend and the bridge between her past and present, gestured behind him at the guilt shop's floor of fabric and patterns.

"She was happy. Happier, at least, than she had been. And I had helped a patient. Maybe it was the mad scientist in me," and the wink Dana remembered from her first night in the quilt shop returned. "I could never be sorry."

Chapter 11

"So, you are not Stanley. You are George?" Margo had to be re-assured.

"Geroge Stanely, at your service," the old man bowed gently.

"Thank you," Dana mouthed between tears.

"It is like we are meeting you again for the first time," Edna said plainly.

"But Stan—, er, George, I mean, Professor," Janet was the first to step through the formalities. "Where are the quilts? The only log cabin here is the one we made together, a class model almost a decade ago." She pointed to the dark wool corner quilt at the end of the picture windows, appliqued with a vine border.

"Yes, and I have never seen a Mariner's Compass quilt here before." Edna declared to everyone.

"Maybe she had to sell them," Margo offered.

"You can't just sell a quilt made in crisis. Not a therapy quilt," Alice's voice seemed to come from experience.

"I can't say. I mean, I've told you all I know," George had nothing more to share.

"These answers are heavy enough," Dana weighed the three letters on the palm of her hand.

"Indeed. Well said," and Janet offered to make Dana a cup of tea.

"No, thank you. I want some time to let this all sink in." Dana's day had been surprising, then warmhearted, and finally, exhausting.

The pizza things were cleared away. The old cheddar quilt was rehung over the now-empty china cupboard. Little remained of the day's adventure except for a deeper hue of friendship in the air, and the group's newly bound quilts, of course.

Everyone got a hug as they departed.

George was the last to leave. After a long hug, Dana said, "You have reunited my family—preserved a missing generation."

He paused and considered the flooring. "Or, another way to see it, I kept her from you. She never contacted you out of fear of what would happen to me. Keeping the secret of my involvement made her a bit recluse."

George leaned heavily on his cane, still carrying the burden of secrets. "'Bridges crossed,' that's what Angie would say whenever I tried to talk of renewing options. I am glad to tell my story finally."

"Well, I'm not sorry," Dana assured the old man. "And I'm not the type to change my mind about that. You'll see."

"Then, you are staying?" George asked, with obvious hope in his eyes.

"I haven't quite decided that," said Dana thoughtfully, "But I know I will never be far away from Aunt Angie's friends. Or from her knight in shining armor." It was Dana's turn to redeem a parting wink.

Her understanding moved George. It was evident he had waited many years for that reassurance. He left with his hand on his heart and a lighter step beside his cane.

Dana again waited for the tiny bell above the door announcing the departure of her latest guests to finish ringing. The shop was filled with nightfall yet warmed by the quilts hanging above. Her shop was cozy. My shop? Indeed, her very own quilt shop, with a cheerful air remaining behind from the bustle of the quilters. Dana was glad she had let them in after all.

Was this what it meant to be a quilt shop owner: continual alterations? Could Dana accept this quieter lifestyle on a dead-end street? Or would it always be Great-Aunt Angie's store, first and foremost? No harm in selling out to someone new and returning to her regular lifestyle. She could always visit Aunt Angie's friends, right?

At the end of the shop, the highest hanging quilt began to sway, stirred by an evening breeze. As Dana watched the quilt, triangles shifted into squares, and grays melded into peacock blue and back again. Presumably, her aunt had created this artful covering, along with all the rest of the quilts in the shop and many more that had gone as gifts, stocked the upstairs apartment, or been sold. How could anyone possibly have that much time? Why would anyone "keep quilting?"

The big blue quilt stirred again. Dana realized then that it shouldn't be moving. Since she could not see any open windows in the rafters, Dana realized,

There must be an attic!

The anticipation of a new adventure revived Dana. She hurried up the twisty stairs and searched Aunt Angie's apartment for the first time. The stair landing was fashioned into the tiniest living room possible. There was only a cozy chair, accompanied by a teacup-sized table, across from a low bookcase with a television. Angie set the three letters and the music box on the bookcase.

They could rest safely there until she packed them to go home with her. The corner kitchen had a cook-top, fridge, and pantry. A center butcher block counter doubled as a dining table with two low-backed stools.

The bathroom and adjacent bedroom were to the immediate left of the stairs. No extra closet or ceiling hatch was immediately noticeable. But the bed sure looked warm and peaceful, and Dana changed her mind again, deciding further escapades should wait until the sun rose again.

As Dana worked her toothbrush and got into her pajamas, she made a mental list of where the morning would go. She needed to find the business files and the attic door—if there was one. And, oh yeah, this velvet-roped key around her neck. It must go to something up here. The attic door, perhaps?

When Dana snuggled under the star quilt and turned out the bedside lamp, she was again enveloped in purple light. She chuckled to herself. After everything, they had never found the switch for the neon QUILTS light. Add it to the list, she told herself.

Yet another point on the list of things to find: breakfast.

The bookcase in the sitting room held only quilting books; there were no business reports. Likewise, no files were in the drawers beneath the cash register station. Dana walked through the empty shop, as she had done the day before in her PJs and Aunt Angie's bathrobe. She said good morning to each of Great-Aunt Angie's quilts, taking a moment to appreciate the changes wrought by daybreak upon the character of the stitches. Soon, hope for breakfast overtook her, and Dana decided it was time to explore the world outside the quilt shop.

It was a cable knit and crows kind of day. Although she planned on grabbing a quick breakfast, Dana opted for a small-town diner and a plate of proper pancakes and bacon. All the comforts of a homemade breakfast, only as far away as her city-slick books could take her and closer to downtown than QUILTS. Dana sat comfortably at the diner counter. The townspeople around her wore plaid against the autumn morn.

While Dana was awaiting a refill pitcher of heated maple syrup, she began to feel stares from the red-topped tables behind her. Dana checked that her cardigan buttons were aligned. Was her hair uncombed, like yesterday morning when she met the quilt class? The shiny backsplash of the diner's counter showed Dana she was indeed properly arranged this morning. So, Dana returned her focus to the pancakes.

It wasn't long before a lady from the corner table approached with a mug in hand and sat at the bar stool next to Dana. "We heard about your aunt's funeral. Sorry for staring. We want to say, 'Welcome.'"

Dana's face was full of pancakes, so she only nodded appreciation to the stranger. Turning, she waved to the tables behind her.

"So, do you have new plans for QUILTS? My name is Jane, by the way."

Dana was glad this turned out to be a friendly town. "Hi Jane, glad to know you. Are you a quilter?"

"Anyone who met Angie became a quilter," Jane confided, sipping from her mug. "Towns full of quilters."

Dana smiled. From what she had learned the night before, she could absolutely believe Aunt Angie recruited quilters everywhere she went. "To tell the truth, Jane, since you asked, there is more to consider in my planning than just running a new business. I'm starting to appreciate what a complicated art quilting is. Plans will depend on what I find today," Dana said as much to herself as to Jane.

An heirloom breeze led the way as Dana walked home between turning leaves and misty pumpkin-scented paths. She received more condolences from passing townsfolk who recognized a stranger with a family resemblance to the quilt shop owner. Most wanted to know if the quilt shop was staying open. Some told of quilts they were working on. Dana felt she understood their enthusiasm, even if she couldn't picture their endeavors.

All around her, the autumn vibe was plum, pumpkin, and a paler honey gold. *What a lovely quilt these colors would make.* Dana suspected she, too, was catching whatever spell Aunt Angie had weaved into the town. And what would you call that green, the last remnant of summertime on a piece of lawn peeking through a heap of fallen leaves? *Is that olive, or maybe sage? Is there a fabric to match that back at the shop?* Dana suspected she had seen such a color on the last range of bolts. Oh dear.

Stopping outside QUILTS, Dana looked up at the building, trying to place where an attic would be. She was sure the blue quilt hanging from the rafters couldn't have been moving alone. She needed to find the source of the drafts. Dana hoped she could also locate her great-aunt's missing business records.

Clouds were graying above the shingles. Could the attic entrance be hidden behind another quilt, like the cheddar Broken Dishes? *What would be the appropriate quilt to hide an attic window?* Dana wondered.

Dana easily located her bedroom window beneath the brightly lit neon sign. Crunching through fallen leaves, she circled the property to the East side of the shop. This was an experience rarely encountered in her palm tree studded California homeland. Dana paused in her search to hop on a small pile of leaves collected by the fall breeze, reveling in the satisfying crackle of the dried leaves.

The back of the shop was equally gratifying. It showed the expected clerestory windows around the showroom, with something new: two eyebrow dormer windows.

Chapter 13

Dana went to the cutting table. "I need a yardstick, like the one mounted on this table," she called out jokingly. She reached underneath the table to where she had found the spool of velvet ribbon the night before. Sure enough, there was a yardstick in the cubbyhole. Dana smiled without questioning the acquisition.

In the upstairs apartment, Dana measured walls, hoping to find extra spaces where an attic entrance could be hidden. She moved throw-rugs to search for trap doors. Inside the wardrobe, she found sweaters—nice sweaters, in fact. She paused her search to try some on.

The studio apartment was cozy but sparse. There wasn't room to hide anything—just the essentials: a few dishes, two pots and a frying pan, and a few toiletries, all in their correct places. A kitchen cupboard held pasta, crackers, cans of soup, and pantry things. *Wait—if pantry things are in the cupboards, what is in the pantry?*

Next to the fridge, inline between the kitchen and the sitting room, was the pocket door Dana had assumed last night to enclose a pantry. She set her yardstick against the door moulding and read-ied the brass key hanging around her neck. But the door wasn't locked, and its tab handle slid the door easily. She stepped through the slim opening.

Only a few broad white wooden steps formed a split-level stair-case filled with the scant sunlight of the graying day. Dana skirted some bulk pantry items stored in the threshold space as she ascend-ed into a low, slant-roofed room sided with two dormer windows.

Open framings shelved with quilts flanked the entrance. Only the end wall was paneled in beadboard. A few suitcases were stacked at the end of the attic. There were no dusty trunks or old toys, no puddles of holiday decorations awaiting their return season. Everything was ship-shaped and as organized as the shop downstairs. The space Dana found was not a dusty attic at all. It was an office.

Between the two windows resided a desk cozy with plaid lampshades, an antique swivel bankers' chair, and the scent of lilacs. Cooler than the rest of the building, this was the space that had called to her by moving the big quilt hung from the ceiling downstairs. Dana spread her arms and spun around in the higher center of the attic.

It does exist!

The desk was small. It could have been a vanity table in a former life. Inside the drawers, Dana found ledgers: taxes, vendor accounts, bank books, and inventory. There was even a calendar of planned classes and promotions, with budgets included. The missing books were as easy to hand as if she had pulled them from the cutting table.

Chapter 14

In a framing gap between the windows, Dana found a shelf of albums with photos of past quilting classes. Sitting at the desk and turning the scrapbooks, she saw the younger selves of Edna and Alice, with earlier quilts among strangers, all past students of Aunt Angie.

There was Aunt Angie herself. Dana only knew the outlines of her face and bohemian hairstyle from the pictures at the funeral. But these were more like action pictures. She saw her long-lost family standing arm in arm with friends. Here, holding up a quilt block, and there, leading a class at the now familiar cutting table. Dana tried to imagine herself in these pictures, a quilt shop owner the likes of Great-Aunt Angie.

A slow spattering rain brought Dana's attention back to the attic office. Sitting at the desk, Dana could view a watercolor version of the treetops and taller buildings downtown through the two dormer windows.

So this was Aunt Angie's life after the asylum. She was recognized around town. She quilted daily downstairs in her quilt shop at the end of a quiet street. In the evenings, she retired upstairs to a cozy apartment. And for business, she had a proper and peaceful office with a glorious view. Dana's hand traced the waterfall edge of the boudoir desk. Could a girl want anything more?

Dana hunted in the desk until she found a matchbox for lighting a candle on the corner of the desk, thereby revealing the source of the lilacs in the room. She sat for a long while watching the candle flame reflected in the rainy windows.

On the plane, Dana had told herself that this funeral trip was a family duty. But on the other side of that coin was the unexpected gift of a business to run. A specialty business requiring a passion and talent that Dana was unfamiliar with. When should you take on someone else's cause? Or Curse? Or their saving grace?

At last, Dana drew out her cell phone and dialed her West Coast life.

"Gato d'Oro Winery." The fact that her boss, Marjorie, was answering the phone herself told Dana everything she needed to know about the situation at her job.

"Hello, Marjorie," Dana asked anyway, "How are things?"

"Hair on fire," Marjorie was always blunt but rarely exaggerated to this extent. "When are you coming back?"

"Actually, I need to extend this trip a few more days."

"Oh Dana, I understand, it must be tough, services and all that. But how can I launch this season's wine tasting without my events coordinator?"

"Well, I made sure Denise had everything needed for the event before I left, just in case. I know she's new, but I'm sure she can handle it."

"Denise is younger than you are," Marjorie was borderline exasperated.

"If you wish, I'll call Manny at Wide Creek Cellars. I'm sure he won't mind checking up on things." And taking my job, Dana finished to herself.

"There are still things that I need answers for here." Dana closed her eyes, "I wish things could stand still for a moment so I can make some decisions."

"Well, while you're standing still, our launch is this weekend, and I need you here." Marjorie was sounding more and more like her hair really was on fire. Dana gave her space in the conversation to recover.

"Oh, alright," Marjorie relented. "Have Manny call me. I expect he can be on hand for Denise's last-minute emergencies at least."

"I'll get back as soon as possible," Dana closed with more reassurance than she felt. Manny, she knew, was gifted at making opportunities for himself. He could easily move into her job by rescuing Marjorie this weekend. Maybe she should pack and go home, despite what she had told Marjorie.

But before calling Manny, Dana searched the quilts stacked between the framing at the attic door. One shelf had small quilts; the rest were big enough to cover the day bed. Some Dana recognized from the picture albums; these must be the class models. But none resembled the log cabin letter or the compass music box.

Dana changed her flight to the end of the week. Then she called California again to reach her colleague, Manny. In the end, Manny was out, so Dana could only leave him a message.

One last thing to do before closing the office: Dana retrieved the music box and letters from beside the television and gave them a new home on the attic desk. She took time to reread the matron's letter. Smiling, Dana recalled Edna's pride in the impact Angie's first quilt had on her old....roommates? What did one call their associates in an asylum? What would Angie call them? What did she call the Professor?

Chapter 15

Dana's solitude ended when she heard the bell on the shop door, followed by indistinct women's voices from downstairs. Dana hadn't expected to stay so long upstairs, so she had left the shop door unlocked. Or possibly it was a Freudian Fail, had she subconsciously left it open, hoping one of her new friends would stop by?

Dana rushed to snuff the lilac candle and hurried from the secluded office, sliding the pocket door shut behind her as Mrs. McGinty came onto the apartment landing, followed by a red-manicured stranger in a pink raincoat, carrying a terrier likewise wearing a pink bow.

Dana didn't mask her surprise, "Mrs. McGinty, I thought you had gone back home already."

"There you are, Dana," Miriam McGinty made air kisses in Dana's direction. "I couldn't leave town knowing you were stuck with.... with this," and she shook her umbrella toward the shop downstairs. "I've brought you help. This is Alana Perkins. She knows everything about quilt shops and has several already. She can fix all of this for you."

Alana Perkins reached the top of the stairs and set her tiny dog down to run around Dana's feet.

"How do you do?" stammered Dana. Could it be that easy, a ready buyer? She should have waited to call Marjorie at the winery.

Alana turned, evaluating the apartment before addressing Dana in a low voice, "So you are Angie's niece,"

"Yes, did you know my great-aunt?"

"I am acquainted.... with your shop," Alana answered slowly.

Dana didn't know why, but she was nervous about having the women in Aunt Angie's apartment. She moved toward the stairs, "Come downstairs again," she invited over her shoulder, "I can show you around," as if she knew where anything was. But Miriam, Alana, and the dog stayed where they were.

"No need. I'm sure you'll find my offer acceptable." Alana insisted.

"Yes, acceptable." Mrs. McGinty chirped in agreement.

Dana spread her hands, palms up, and shrugged. "I'm not sure if I am selling," she explained, almost apologetically.

"Nonsense," Mrs. McGinty was sure. "This is not your life, Dana. What do you know about running a shop, and one with this specialty to boot?"

Thunder sounded above them, and the rain beat a little harder on the roof of the tiny apartment.

"There are many logistical concerns in a shop like this," Alana Perkins embarked on an explanation, high heels clicking on the linoleum as she stepped around the kitchen island to pick up her pink bowed dog. "Wholesale vendors and jobbers, payment terms, inventory by item and by yardage, international trade markets, budgets, training staff and teachers...I wouldn't expect you to be aware of all this, Dana."

As the winery's events coordinator, Dana worked with vendors, budgets, and the odd regional market. Yet, she never did anything on this scale and didn't want to admit it. If Aunt Angie had taught herself everything about quilting, then Dana could also.

"Suppose I liquidate—fire sale. Clear everything out. Then, sell the building. Walk away." And with that, Dana continued down the twisty little staircase, forcing her surprised quests to follow her to the darkening shop floor. A parting glance over her shoulder showed the Perkins lady stiffen and clench her dog who contributed a tiny yelp.

"Be reasonable, Dana," Mrs. McGinty called after her as she fumbled to catch up on the stairs. Selling to Alana would be much simpler and faster. You could go home tomorrow. Wait, Dana."

On the last step, Dana thought she heard the shop bell again and turned to see the door shutting. Has Miriam brought someone else?

Dana stood in front of the cash register as she had on her first night following the funeral, but now she felt like she was in a maze. Mrs. McGinty was far too anxious regarding Dana's affairs. Someone unknown had just left the shop, Dana was sure. Who was this stranger, Alana Perkins, and her little dog too?

"Miriam," Dana grabbed Mrs. McGinty's elbow and drew her near for a close word. "What's in this for you?"

"Me?" Mrs. McGinty was more annoyed than surprised. "Why, I..." she couldn't locate a coherent explanation.

Holding her little terrier, Alana Perkins was descending the twisty staircase like a runway model.

"Don't you think we should acknowledge Miriam's contribution in bringing us together? A percentage of the sale price, perhaps, as a thank you," she declared as she reached the floor. "Such an odd building. The sound does travel," and Alana again loosed her little dog to prowl the shop floor.

Dana rolled her eyes.

"Dana, I only want to help...." Miriam tried to substantiate her presence there, but Dana cut short her protestations.

"Why do I need help? All I have to do is hang out a sale sign and call a realtor. Anyone can do that."

"Truly," Alana nodded cautiously. "But there is a good chance you may overlook something...anything of value."

Instinctively, Dana's hand went to the velvet ribbon around her neck. "For example?"

"Well, some of these quilts might be worth... something," Alana shrugged and sounded skeptical as she gestured toward the large quilts above them. The terrier ran to bark at the rain cascading over the shop's front casement windows.

"You are right," Dana sounded triumphant. "I need an auction, not a fire sale. An auctioneer, with a proper appraisal." She strode to the door and held it open. The rain tinted by the neon light splashed purple on her boots. "I'm sure you'll hear when QUILTS estate sale is scheduled," and she didn't care how cold her voice sounded to her unexpected and unwanted guests.

"Well, I don't appreciate the delay, but as I will surely be the sole bidder, I will pay far less for this place in the end. Bargello, come!" Alana Perkins scooped up the terrier and headed out into the early evening rain with Mrs. McGinty and her umbrella rushing to catch up.

Chapter 16

Dana let the shop door slide to meet the rain. She dragged a bolt of red cloth from a range of fabrics and dropped it on the floor with a satisfying muffled thump. Sitting on the bolt, she pulled off her boots and crossed her legs. End-cap patterns swayed above her head. She reached up past the patterns and pulled a basket of fabric rolls into her lap.

The nerve! Mrs. Mcginty brings a stranger right into her home. Insulting her quilts and trying to take her shop. Wait- don't I mean Aunt Angie's shop? Dana chastised herself. She should not have been so rude - was she rude? Indeed, she should not have matched their rudeness. She should have been a better host. A ready-made offer, an answer that walked right in all on its own, a way out of the burden of this gift. Why couldn't I have just said, 'Thank you?'

Why the duality issues? Aunt Angie was gone; this was her shop now. Dana had every right to be insulted by Alana Perkins' takeover. Except, what had she done to earn this place, this very spot, here on the floor? Dana looked around the now darkened shop, with the purple glow of rain over her shoulder from the large front windows. In every direction, quilts and the accouterments of future quilts. Only the classroom with the kitchenette and mysterious cutting table beneath the apartment rested in complete darkness.

Aunt Angie had -quite literally- escaped her troubles, learned to quilt, built a home and a business, plus a lot of quilts. What had Dana done? She had never even met her great-aunt. Of course, she had shown up when family duty called. Does that count for something?

Dana found she was tossing a fabric bun between her hands. Tied with a ribbon, it had a fanned edge like a truncated deck of cards. "Jelly Roll,'" the tag declared. It had a comforting weight even though it fit easily in Dana's hand. Dana cast the cut fabric wheel down the wooden floor. It wobbled a bit whenever it hit the bow, but it rolled fairly true into the dark of the classroom.

Dana selected another bun to roll but stopped when she saw the first returning from the classroom. Rolling slowly toward her, the Jelly Roll turned toward the door and finished its run lodged beneath the first range of bolts.

This place is crooked. Dana decided there must be a slope on the floor. An appraisal may not be the best plan, as it could uncover as many flaws as treasures. She would go upstairs, make a cup of soup, get a quilt book from the shelves under the TV, and take them both to bed. In the morning, she would be an adult and make a decision already.

Dana's fingers brushed against something cold and metallic as she reached under the range to retrieve the Jelly Roll. Intrigued, she moved closer to her knees, illuminating the space with her cell phone flashlight. The Jelly Roll had been stopped in its arc by a metal box bolted to the floor, a heavy-duty toggle switch on top.

Impulsively, Dana flipped the heavy switch. The purple light disappeared. She tried the switch again. In a moment, the purple light returned. Without thinking, she had found it at last, the industrial light switch for the neon QUILTS sign. Of course, it was a floor switch. Close to the door, Aunt Angie would have stepped on the toggle to shut off the sign when she closed the shop and vice versa when opening.

Dana shut the light off again. QUILTS was now officially closed. A weak moonlight moving through the storm clouds filled the shop with enough light for Dana to re-shelve the Jelly Roll basket and red fabric. She picked up her boots and finally locked the door. She started up the apartment stairs. But Dana stopped on the second step and turned to review the cloth kingdom of the quilt shop. "Thank you, Aunt Angie," she called into the darkness before continuing upstairs to bed.

Chapter 17

Upstairs, the apartment was extra dark without the previously ubiquitous purple glow. The rain was at last settling into a peaceful drizzle and inspired Dana to take a long soaking shower before getting into her pajamas. She then kept to her plan of making soup and choosing a quilt book for bedtime reading. The soup turned out to be celery; in the dark, she had mistaken it for chicken. Fortunately, Aunt Angie's kitchen stocked Dana's favorite tiny oyster crackers, so the unexpected soup was a success after all.

Dana skipped the kitchen island stools and chose the wing-backed chair across from the bookcase for enjoying her dinner. The side table was only large enough for her mug. Under the chair, she discovered a tuffet. *It seems we like the same things*, Dana mused about Aunt Angie's home as she doubled-down on cozy, stretching her legs on the tiny ottoman, hearing the rain drizzle on the slates above while the hot soup filled her with renewed warmth. Dana was content and grateful for the Goldilocks-sized home.

It had been a big day. She had found the light switch for the neon QUILTS sign. Also, meeting the town, calling California, the storm... Dana looked for a distraction to stop her counting down through the day's events to the unwanted visitors, Mrs. Mcginty and Alana Perkins. What else did Aunt Angie enjoy? What shows did she watch? Are there quilting shows? Dana assumed there must be.

Dana moved to sit on the floor before the bookshelf. The book covers were varied in their style of quilts, yet all promised to make quilting easy. Which one would be Aunt Angie's favorite? Dana decided to look for the most used book, but all the covers were well warn.

So far, Dana's quilting education had been chaotic and quick, but she felt she could recognize a log cabin quilt, like the form of the Matron's letter. To end the day, she would search the shelves for a log cabin book. Her efforts revealed three books with log cabin quilts on the covers.

Not in any rush, Dana compared the books page by page while finishing her soup. Laying on the floor like she used to do with her homework, Dana studied quilting. Seam Allowance: an extra ¼" added to each edge of a patch. Block: could be any size, depending on the number and size of logs (rectangular patches), but all blocks must match in size. Base Patch: each log cabin block begins with a center square, traditionally red, to mark the cabin's hearth.

The calculations of patches appealed to Dana, but the magic was in color placement. The alignment of dark versus light fabrics gave facets to the simple log cabin block's possibilities: Courthouse Steps, Barn Raising, Sunshine & Shadows, Fields & Furrows, Lanterns, and Tulips. There was even a star quilt and a heart quilt created from log cabin blocks.

Dana was pleased with herself. She understood Aunt Angie's first quilt. There was only one log cabin variation Dana couldn't comprehend: the Pineapple. So, she chose Easy Log Cabins to take to bed with her. Maybe she could figure it out before falling asleep. Dana replaced the other books and headed to bed.

But once tucked in under the star quilt, with the inviting pillow, Dana forgot the book on the nightstand. As she drifted off to sleep, a piece aligned in her memory of the rainy night. The sound of the bell and the door closing as she headed down the stairs ahead of Mrs. McGinty. Someone had been in the shop beside the three women upstairs and... oh yeah... Bargello, too.

Chapter 18

In the morning, Dana awoke when she heard a book fall in the living room. I must not have reshelved them well enough last night. Via yawning and stretching, she made her way out of bed and down the short route to the landing/living room. There was indeed a book on the floor, but as Dana returned it to the bookcase, she found it was not one of the log cabin titles which had fallen onto the floor. This book had a dark cover and was extra warn. Crazy Quilts of the Victorian Era, the title read.

She had only been kidding when she asked the cutting table for a yardstick. Standing on the stairs the evening before, she had been sincere when she thanked Aunt Angie -for the quilt shop. After discovering the industrial light switch, the place suddenly felt her own. But this, a gift book, a book selected... by Aunt Angie?

Dana tossed the book to the wing-backed chair and hurried to dress and leave the shop. She carried her boots and comb, but as she passed the chair, she couldn't resist grabbing the Crazy Quilts book and stuffing it in her bag. Breakfast would sort everything out. She had to get to a place where she could think.

Downstairs, Dana hopped into her boots, unlocked the shop door, and backed out while fishing in her purse for keys. She jumped when she backed into the group of friends waiting at the door. A brisk wind further tussled Dana's unkempt hair and muddled the words of everyone talking at once.

"Thank goodness you are still here!" exclaimed Janet.

"I hadn't meant to eavesdrop," blurted Margo.

"Give the girl some room," Alice was animated, waving her arms.

Dana dropped her bag on the sidewalk and held her comb in front of her like a wand. "Stop," she commanded.

All the ladies froze in place.

"I just need a moment," Dana said, defiantly battling the wind and tangled hair with her comb as the quilt ladies stared.

Momentarily, the tangles won, and Dan gave up, stamping her boot as she stuffed the comb into her purse. She turned to Edna and said, "Take me to the place where you got the donuts."

Edna shrugged, her palms up. "I don't have a car."

"We'll go in my truck," Janet was already leading the way across the street to her big red truck.

❈❈❈

The wind continued its wailing all around the bakery, occasionally splattering leaves against the windows and snatching the covers from pink donut boxes of customers leaving with their treats. With everyone fitted in a corner booth, Janet began the explanation again. "We were waiting to talk with you Dana, because, well, we heard you might be selling the quilt shop."

"But everyone knew that," Dana couldn't see where this talk was going.

"Right," Janet tried again, looking to each of her friends, "We...heard you were considering selling to Alana Perkins."

"There was someone else in the shop!" Dana blurted out the puzzle of the night before.

"It was me-e-e," Margo was wringing her hands and speaking very fast. "I didn't mean to listen in! You see, I remembered that we hadn't vacuumed after quilt class, and I didn't want you to be stuck with all our threads on the floor, so I thought I would pop in and say 'hi' and do some tidying up. But when I came in, there was yelling upstairs, and I was deciding what to do. I just ran out when I heard voices coming down the stairs." Margo finished, her story at last exhausted. She took a deep breath, relieved at the telling of her faux pas.

"Yes, well," Edna picked up the story. "We understand you have a huge decision to make, Dana. So we decided to share with you, ah, local business, yes, public knowledge that you wouldn't know about. Since you are new here."

Alice nodded and looked around the donut shop to see if anyone else could overhear them. "Alana Perkins," Alice confided in hushed tones, "owns all the quilt shops in every town along the river-—except here."

Dana's only thought was de ja vu. Here she was again, with donuts, coffee, and messed up hair, the same as the last time she met this group of ladies. The scowl knitting her eyebrows together said this was becoming a strange habit.

"You see," Janet tried again. "Once Alana owns all the quilt shops, nothing will stop her. She can—she will—raise all the prices."

"Sure, you can buy fabric online. But it's not the same as feeling it at the shop." Edna was adamant.

"You can print PDF patterns, which is almost as nice as getting a published one..." Janet continued.

"But when the cat has hidden your last spool of purple thread, or you nick your rotary blade..." Margo jumped in, waving her arms again.

Edna pulled Margo's hands out of the air. "Yes, it's those emergency purchases, the notions, where Alana makes the heaviest price fixing. You do see, don't you, dear?"

They all leaned forward over the table, waiting for a sign of comprehension from Dana. She looked at each of them in turn. Dana started to speak and then shut her mouth. She sat back in the booth and took a swig of coffee. At last, Dana said, "I think the quilt shop is haunted."

Chapter 19

Everyone was talking at once.

"Then you are selling the shop to Alana!" Margo was wailing all over again.

"Haunted by who? You don't mean Angie?" Janet was best at keeping up.

"Look, if you are upset about Margo's eavesdropping..." Alice was hunting for a practical response.

Dana brought the Crazy Quilts book out of her bag and tried explaining how she had found it.

"Anyone need more coffee?" The donut shop waitress in a pink apron and hat stood over the ladies with a fresh pot of coffee.

Edna stood up. "Ladies, please," she commanded, and the gabbing subsided. Yes, we definitely all need more coffee. And some cinnamon rolls, too. Thank you, Cecily," she addressed the waitress on behalf of everyone.

"Mine's tea," corrected Alice.

"I got you," Cecily reassured her as she refilled the coffee cups.

"Ladies," Edna began again. "We need to listen to Dana. She is all alone here and hasn't had anyone to talk with since...the funeral. And our class. And..."

"And Alana Perkins," Margo was close to shouting.

"Yes, alright, we will get to Alana," Edna sat down. "Go ahead, Dana. Tell us, how are you?"

The question stunned Dana. How was she?

"I am... I feel..." Dana's eyes brimmed with tears, and she accepted a napkin from Alice. "I am lost," Dana let it all out between sobs. "I am the last of my family, and I have inherited this beautiful gift, but I'm not qualified to keep it, and I must be back at work this weekend, or I may lose my job. Mrs. McGinty says she is helping me, but Mrs. Perkins was rude, and now you say she is scheming, too. And odd things keep showing up in the quilt shop, but I haven't found my aunt's quilts."

That last part surprised Dana. The shop was full of quilts, on every wall, hanging from the ceiling even, and stacked at the attic/office entry. Why would she be looking for more quilts? Her sobs subsided with the telling, and she blew her nose with the napkin. She smiled wanly. "Thanks, I needed that." Janet patted her hand across the table. Alice put an arm around her and shared a quick hug.

Edna fingered the cover of the Crazy Quilts book. "And... maybe you fear that you might be crazy, like your great-aunt?" Looking at the book, Edna said the quiet part out loud.

"Y-yes." Dana began sobbing all over again. "Because that makes more sense than being haunted." She shared about the moving quilt, finding the ruler, the office, the light switch, and finally, the book. She stopped when she realized five faces were listening to her story. Cecily stood over their table with a plate of cinnamon rolls.

"I know," said Edna, always practical. "Why don't you talk to Professor Stanley? After all, he was a trained psychologist. And, as it turned out, he's known Angela longer than any of us."

"Or," offered Cecily, setting down the warmed cinnamon rolls dripping with icing and butter in the center of the table. "You could have a seance. My cousin Debbie is a Medium."

Chapter 20

In the end, Dana accepted both suggestions. Over the next few days, she busied herself setting up the quilt shop for the seance. Events were her forte, and the party planning made her feel more at home. The quilt class joined in the bustle, offering supplies and chauffeuring Dana to all the best secondhand shops.

Everywhere they went, Dana was welcomed by people who had known Aunt Angie or had at least visited QUILTS. When the news of the impending seance came up, many people shared their own ghost stories. Some even reported strange happenings at QUILTS.

"It's just an old building in an old New England town. Stories like this practically grow in the pumpkin patches. Don't let them spook you," Edna cautioned.

With silver spray paint, Dana transformed old lamps and trays into a Hollywood Regency ambiance. Velvet shawls covered the shop's windows. Pumpkins and corn stalks came to decorate the sidewalk in front of the quilt shop. Per Medium Debbie's instructions, racks of bolts were moved, and the cutting table was rolled to the center of the quilt shop and circled by chairs.

Dana avoided the attic and the cutting table as she worked, but she kept the Crazy Quilt book nearby. In free moments, she would browse its pages and wonder at the countless stitching varieties and fancy fabrics pictured within. The dark fabrics held a fascination for her; they were always used in tiny pieces and somehow haphazardly united. Dana was sure each patch told a story.

Riding in the back of the Uber had been one, probably the last, of these free moments. Dana closed the book and returned it in her handbag as the car rolled through the cemetery. "Here will be fine," she let the driver know as she saw Professor Stanley waiting ahead, his back turned to the road. She didn't want his solitude intruded on by the car. Plus, walking would delay the conversation she was now beginning to regret initiating. "No need to stay," Dana sent the car away and waited until it had almost exited the cemetery grounds before approaching Professor Stanely at her great-aunt's graveside.

The first time Dana had come here, the leaves had fallen in abundant color. Now, the trees were bare, and the ground held a damp that clawed up at the fringes of her secondhand store scarf. Dana slung her bag over her shoulder, jammed her hands into her jacket pockets, took a deep breath, and let her feet follow the path through the gray headstones to Professor Stanley.

George turned at the sound of her steps and leaned more heavily on his cane. He wore an old driving cap that gave his face a boyish appearance. Alice was right; Dana supposed he must have been handsome as an intern, and then she stopped herself. Who cared? He was just an old man now.

"Dana, hello, I'm glad you called," Professor Stanley began.

"Thank you for meeting me," Dana's voice sounded colder than she intended. She shivered and folded her scarf tighter.

Professor Stanley nodded but said nothing more. A wistful smile settled on his face.

"I don't know what I wanted," Dana said into the silence between them. "Just to say goodbye, I suppose. As you knew my great-aunt best, it seemed right."

"To say goodbye—to your aunt?" the Professor queried with a tilt of his head.

"No. Maybe. I don't know." Dana was getting irritated by his smug little grin.

The Professor paused for a moment, then brought in a new question. "Where are you going, Dana?"

"You mean, what have I decided about the shop? Everyone keeps asking me that."

"I think we both mean, where are you going, in life?" The Professor's voice was gentle, but it still annoyed Dana.

"Hey, I didn't ask for this gift, or for the family duty, or whatever." Dana stepped back but found her path blocked by tombstones.

"It's all these strange things," she blurted out. "Things just showing up. Coming to me. Bringing answers that I didn't know I cared about." She wheeled on the Professor. "And where are my Aunt Angie's quilts, the early ones she made before the shop? Tell me that!"

The Professor's only reaction was to stand straighter with both hands on his cane.

"I'm sorry, Professor, I don't know why I am shouting." Dana shrugged and looked at the sky, trying not to cry.

The Professor's answer was simple and sure, "It is because you are grieving."

"That's silly." Dana tried to argue even though a piece of his words rang true in her heart. "How can you grieve someone you've never met?"

"How do you say goodbye to someone you've never met?" George replied.

Exasperated, Dana hung her head.

"Walk with me," he said, starting across the rows of headstones, ignoring the path. His cane swung lightly over the damp earth. "Look around us," George motioned with his cane. "Fall is the season for letting things go."

The walking was nudging the sudden, mysterious anger from her head. "You're saying I need to let Aunt Angie go?"

"You can do whatever you want." George made it sound so simple. "Do you want to hold onto the past? Make sense of it? Or make it go away?" He paused to turn toward her. "But whatever you decide, Dana, something will have to go. You can't keep all those things. That's why I suggested we meet here," and he resumed his stroll. "This is the best time, and the best place, for letting things go."

Dana found herself stopped in her tracks. Darn, the little man was right. She had been so focused on what to pick and what obligations were owed. She hadn't even considered what she needed to release.

"Professor," Dana caught up to him. "There is a seance at QUILTS tonight."

"Ha - I think the whole town has heard about that," he replied.

"You are welcome to come, if you want to," Dana offered the invitation by way of apology for her earlier temper. "Do you, ah, believe in ghosts, Professor?"

He turned a brilliant smile on her. "I believe," he answered as if to a classroom of students, "that ghosts are a relic from our lizard brain, the *basal ganglia*. Perhaps a primordial association, an instinct long defunct, nothing more. My dear friend Angie is here," he nodded at the plot behind them. George placed a gloved hand over his heart. "And she will always be here."

Dana took his arm as they strolled through the cemetery.

"You know," said the Professor. "You look a lot like her."
Now Dana couldn't help smiling. "Thanks, Professor."

Chapter 21

It wasn't quite dark yet, but a fog was already rising. Dana couldn't wait to turn on the neon QUILTS sign. She stepped on the heavy switch with her platform shoes, then ran outside to watch the purple sign light up. This was the first time she had turned it on to announce that QUILTS was open, welcoming one and all. Her silver gown reflected the fog as she bounced around the sidewalk, clapping and giggling, the brass key on its red velvet lanyard hiding in the silken cowl that draped her shoulders and scooped low around the backless gown.

As hostess, Dana was in her element. Tonight, she was the quilt shop owner. Tomorrow, she will likely have to sell everything. But for this one night, it was all hers, and she was raring to enjoy every minute of it. On her way back inside, Dana high-fived a scarecrow holding a "Seance Tonight" sign.

Inside the quilt shop, a 1930s hit parade was already playing via some speakers borrowed from Margo's grandson: Duke Ellington, Benny Goodman, Billie Holiday, and Bing Crosby, of course. The cutting table was draped in purple velvet and black lace, ornamented with Madame Debbie's paraphernalia. There was a tambourine, a brass bell shaped like a pilgrim woman, a silver candelabra, and a vial of salt. Dana was tickled pink to see the traditional clear crystal ball on an ornately tarnished stand, as it made everything complete. Debbie had set four large red glassed lanterns on pillars to define the seance area.

Edna, always the first to arrive, wore black and pearls, as she had for Angie's funeral. Madame Debbie arrived next with her cousin, Cecily, and a co-worker from the donut shop. The girls were enlisted to serve canapes and drinks. They dressed as 1930s cigarette girls, and Janet had brought a matching dress form mannequin for collecting hats and scarves. Janet herself arrived in a tea-length red dress with tulip sleeves, gathered into a red sequin star at the midriff.

Dana waited at the door to greet everyone. She preferred to meet her guests outside, but the night was growing cold quickly, and people just wanted to get indoors. The attendance was overwhelming. Dana was glad to see Nancy, whom she had met at the Diner her first morning in town. And there were many locals Dana had met at the antique shops and the "packie." Margo and her husband swept in with the crowd, sporting matching tuxedos. Margo flourished her Garbo-styled top hat for Dana, but wouldn't give it up to the dress form hat stand. "It's so much fun to wear, I think I'll just keep it with me."

Alice came in wearing a silk novelty print gown featuring lobsters, al a Schiaparelli. She readily stepped in to take over Dana's hostess duties as Dana was called away to organize a second row of chairs to accommodate the unexpected crowd.

When the shop was full to the seams, and the canapes had almost disappeared, Dana rose to the third step on the stairs and tapped her cocktail glass with a pair of shears. The melodic ringing brought everyone's attention and silence.

"I am honored that so many of you came here tonight to remember my Aunt Angie and this place, QUILTS, that -I have learned through meeting some of you- has been a community fixture. Maybe after the seance, I will have some news about the shop's status for you."

"Have you seen any strange things happen here at QUILTS?" Indeed, townsfolk nodded to each other. "I invite you to write your episode on a card and add it to the fishbowl at the checkout stand. I would love to share your experiences."

"Now, to help us explore these unusual happenings, I am honored to host Madam Debbie, a local medium who will help us talk with those on the other side. But before she takes over, I sincerely want to say thanks again. I know that we are having fun tonight with some costumes and treats, but in all sincerity, you knew my Great-Aunt Angela, whereas I never did. Joining me here tonight, for whatever happens next, will help me find closure. And maybe we can help someone from the other side too. Please welcome, Madam Debbie."

From out of the darkened classroom flowed a multitude of feather-fringed organza, bearing the Rubenesque Debbie onto the quilt shop floor. She curtsied to Dana and then to the guests. "I am Madame Deb-O-Rah. I will lead what spirits are gathered here amongst us tonight, to speak through myself," Deborah crossed her arms over her chest, "and tell us how we can help them to cross over." Debbie turned her ample frame, facing each group of guests as she spoke.

"Some spirits are trapped here to finish their purpose, some remain for love, and many are forgetful souls who cannot find their way. With your cooperation," and her glance around the room dared anyone to defy her will, "we will discern which we may so humbly assist."

Chapter 22

"This is, oh my, such a large group." Debbie seemed to notice the townsfolk for the first time. "Never mind- I will ask each of you to participate. Please take a candle or a crystal," she indicated the cigarette girl trays, now replaced with votives.

"Hold your votive in front of you as you pass by each of the four pillars," Deborah instructed, indicating the red-glassed lamps. "Counterclockwise, please!" And Ethel Waters sang Stormy Weather from the speakers as the jumble of neighbors sorted itself into a river cheerfully circling the room.

Madame Deborah spread her arms wide and turned slowly in a circle, pausing to bow toward each red lantern.

"Everyone, please leave your votive on this table as you choose a seat," and she indicated the double row of chairs encircling the table with the sweeping gesture of a game show model. "Dana, you will sit by me."

Next, Deborah lit the candlesticks on the cutting table and called for the shop lights to be turned off. The casement windows covered in random velvet glowed purple at the edges from the neon sign outside in the fog. At last, Deborah moved to the silver-painted dining chair at the head of the adorned cutting table, taking three deep breaths before sitting down.

Dana smiled as she swished the mermaid train of her silken gown to sit at Debbie's right side. Everyone was having such a good time. She could leave this town with satisfaction, knowing she had become part of its story. Dana was contributing a piece to Aunt Angie's legacy, something fun to remember beyond the recent discovery of her secret history of insanity, or at least incarceration.

Deborah raised both arms high. As she lowered them, someone (likely Cecily) turned down the music. The crowd took the hint and likewise moved to silence.

"Please hold hands," Madame Deborah instructed as she started swaying side to side with her eyes closed. "Welcome, Spirits," she intoned slowly in a high monotone pitch. She turned her face to the ceiling. Eyes still closed, Deborah withdrew a small deck of cards from some pocket in her voluminous silken skirts and quickly dealt an arc of thirteen cards.

They weren't cards Dana recognized, a specialized tarot or rune possibly, but she was sure they were all face up even though their dealer worked with her eyes closed. *Debbie has some neat tricks*, Dana mused.

"Dana, the key, it is time," Deborah reached toward Dana with her left hand. Dana removed the velvet rope over her head and placed Aunt Angie's old brass key in the medium's hand.

Deborah rocked back and forth in her seat as she hung the key over the cards. "We call for Angela and for all others who remain here unseen. Spirits, if you can hear me, make yourself known." The key hung straight above the cards.

"We have gathered, hmmm, to help you, hmmm. Tell us, please, what do you need?" Madame Deborah continued rocking and intoning.

"Shake the bell, strike the tambourine, let us hear you. Speak, Spirits, hmmm, choose a card."

So many choices, Dana suspected the spirits would get confused. Holding hands with Janet seated beside her, Dana settled back in her seat and prepared for a long night.

Chapter 23

But she didn't have to wait long, "There, I can see you, Spirit!" Madame Deborah shot her right arm toward a far corner of the room, and everyone turned to look. Simultaneously, the tambourine could be heard rattling on the table, muffled by the velvet covering.

Everyone gasped. Some in the back row of chairs stood for a better look. "Please, remain seated! You must hold hands, don't break the circles," Madame Deborah commanded. *How did she know? She still has her eyes closed.* The tambourine grew louder, bouncing on the table.

"Spirit! Tell us, who are you?" Madame Deborah shouted over the tambourine. Janet's grip tightened on Dana's hand. Dana saw the key swing violently above the cards. Deborah gripped the velvet cord with both hands.

A chilling gust swept the room, guttering the candles. Yelps of astonishment came from the seated guests. The wind was followed by the gentle scent of lilacs creeping into the room, reminding Dana of the attic. *How could Deborah have known about Aunt Angie's lilac candle?*

The key was straining on its cord, pointing to the second card in the arc. Deborah opened her eyes, and Dana saw them shining like small black marbles. "The Fool," she called, barely glancing at the cards. As soon as she spoke, the key swung to aim at the center card. "The Empress," Deborah whispered, bowing her head to her chest, exhausted, yet still holding the key high above The Empress card.

Next, the brass bell rose above the table. Three times it rose, higher each time, seemingly pulled back down, unable to break the grip of gravity. Janet was fairly climbing out of her seat while holding hands with Dana and a wide-eyed Margo on her other side. Dana looked around the room at the surprised and terrified faces of the guests. Edna smirking from the back row was a reassuring sight. *She has probably attended a Madame Deborah seance before.*

On the fourth try, the bell broke free of the table, ringing loudly. The sound aroused Madame Deborah, who began speaking in a creaking voice, "I am here. I am here, for Dana, to see Dana," and Madame Deborah turned her marbled eyes to Dana. Dana found she did not like being called out by ghosts. Whatever she expected of the seance, this was not it.

The tambourine rose to join the bell, and they began circling the table, clamoring, faster and faster, chasing each other, higher and higher, until they were above the heads of the seated guests. Madame Deborah joined the din in her possessed voice, although Dana had stopped listening to whatever inane script she was on.

"Look!" someone shouted. "In front of the windows!" The dress form was moving. It spun a quarter turn, its ruffled skirt swinging. Then it moved a few feet forward, then back toward the door, spinning in a soft dance. People did jump out of their chairs this time.

"Ghost!" Deborah shouted, abandoning her possessed intonation. She stood, tore the stopper out of the salt bottle with her teeth, and flung the contents across the table toward the dancing dress form.

The mannequin, in turn, took off sailing around the shop, banging into the fabric ranges, righting itself, and changing directions.

"Ghost!" Many people were joining Deborah in shouting and pointing. Dana looked for Edna and found her standing on a chair for a better view, scowling with her hands on her hips. *This is not part of the show.*

Dana snatched her key from Madame Debbie's hand and re-hung it around her neck. Then she lifted her long skirt and went after the ghost. Janet scrambled to join her, knocking over Madame Debbie's chair.

The crashing chair was a spark that sent the whole shop into panic. Everyone was up, running to the door, or standing on their chairs. Someone called to turn on the lights, and Cecily answered she was trying, but nothing happened.

Dana reached the far side of the room where the dress form spun round and round in a corner. Dana parried like a linebacker, trying to corner it. The sound of taffeta told Dana that Janet was behind her.

The shop door opened, and the crowd ran out into the street led by Madame Deborah. Cold and purple fog seeped in, replacing them in the jumble of chairs and coasts. The tambourine and bell continued to whirl silently above the table.

The dress form lunged forward, and the ladies screamed and hugged each other. Janet tried to drag her away toward the door when Dana saw a dark spot on the floor moving ahead of the dress dummy. Wherever the spot moved, the dress form followed. When the spot stopped, it seemed to shake.

Dana broke free from Janet and snatched at the spot. A dark cloth came off in her hand, revealing...

"Bargello!" shouted Janet.

Chapter 24

"**N**o, no, no!" An angry voice shouted from the dark classroom corner. "You're just like your aunt; you ruin everything!" The lights came on, and Alana Perkins, dressed in a black jumpsuit and hat, stomped out of her hiding place past the few remaining onlookers who hadn't fled the ghost.

Bargello looked up at Dana, wagging his stubby tail. She stooped down to extricate him from the elaborate harness that linked him to the dress form, still flouncing its ruffles with each beat of his behind.

"Alana Perkins! Have you been hiding there this whole time?" Margo, pointing accusingly at Alana, was still standing on her chair.

Alana glared defiantly at everyone as she pulled the black hat from her head and shook out her gray hair, which settled perfectly coiffed.

"Now there is a real haunting," Dana said under her breath as she delivered Bargello to his owner.

"What did you say?" snapped Alana.

"I said," Dana changed the subject, "Why are you so angry with my great-aunt?"

"Because this is always the fun shop!" Alana was still loudly angry. "I offer lots of classes, but they are never full like Angie's.

"It's true," shrugged Alice, while Margo's husband helped her down from the chair.

"And when I have sales, no one comes. They are all here at Angie's QU-I-L-TS," Alana dragged the shop's name out like it was a bad word.

The remaining guests were staring through their varying degrees of departure, except for one man who had rescued the cigar girl trays and was mixing drinks.

"And when I organize shop hops, even with all my stores, nobody comes except tourists," she whined to Bargello, hugging him close. "Angie should have sold me this shop ages ago. She was the one thing stopping my success."

"Your talents are wasted as an entrepreneur," heads swung to look at Dana, shocked by the sincerity in her voice. "This gear, pulleys," Dana held up the ghost rigging, "it worked amazingly. You should be a designer," she finished handing over the rigging that Alana snatched out of her hands.

"You try designing for these stupid quilters!" Alana waved the contraption toward the group of friends. "They are too cheap to care about real designs. They seldom buy an entire yard of anything. You're even piecing backings now! Worse, you photocopy patterns!" And with her head held high, dog, harness, and hat in hand, Alana stumbled past the jumble of overturned chairs and left Aunt Angie's shop.

"I never copy patterns!" Alice called indignantly after Alana.

"I do," confessed Margo, raising her hand.

"Oh, you shouldn't," counseled Edna, shaking her finger.

Dana shimmied her satin cowl back into place. The guy working the trays handed her a drink, and she slammed it back in one swallow before thanking him. She wanted to smash the glass, but she wasn't sure who it belonged to, so she left it on a nearby chair.

Everyone watched silently as Cecily came in wearing a raincoat over her costume. She went straight to the cutting table and aimed a clicker at the whirling bell and tambourine. The instruments slowed and landed on the table, where Cecily collected them into a bag along with the crystal ball. Grabbing the still-lighted candelabra in her other hand, she left without a word.

"Goodnight, Dana," finally someone broke the quiet, shrugging on their coat. "Nice to meet you, Dana," another waved, heading out the door. "Fun party, we will remember tonight." One by one, the remaining guests departed. Dana waved to each in turn without saying a word. Margo's husband went to bring their car around. Ultimately, the drinks guy signaled he was taking a bottle with him, leaving just Dana and her quilt class girlfriends and the decorated dress form standing alone amongst the party flotsam and jetsam.

"Does this mean Alana won't be buying QUILTS?" Margo wanted to know.

Alice laughed, "You are adorable, Margo," and hugged her friend.

Janet kicked off her heels and leaned back in a chair, stretching her long legs onto the table. "She sure gave my old dress form a workout."

"That was a shock for Debbie," Edna shook her head.

"Then, the whirly, musical things?" Margo pointed at the ceiling, and then along the way Cecily had departed.

"Drone technology," Janet answered. "Like we say in Texas, all hat and no cattle."

"No ghosts. Not tonight," said Edna sympathetically, taking a chair near Janet.

"Well, why didn't the lights work?" Alice sounded defiant as she righted a chair to join the group.

"Alana, again. She was controlling them with the fuse box in the classroom." Dana sat down next to Margo. "Wait, what about the lilacs?"

"What lilacs, Dana?" Edna answered first.

"The smell of lilacs, when the first ghost 'arrived.'" Dana put air quotes around the arrival part.

"Didn't notice," said Margo. And Alice nodded in agreement.

"Someone's perfume?" offered Edna.

"Janet, you were sitting next to me," Dana turned in her chair to face the older woman. "You remember the lilacs, right?"

"Sorry, Dana, I do not."

Silence settled in once again. But it was a close-knit group that sat together after the seance.

"Hey, why is everyone so gloomy?" Alice tried to sound cheerful. "We had fun tonight, right?"

"Yes, I sure did," Margo bounded from her chair. "The whole week, too. It was fun setting up the party, collecting the glassware, decorating, and everything."

Dana nodded, giving herself a mental pat on the back for not breaking Margo's vintage stemware.

"Ha! - I'll never look at my dress form the same, that's for sure!" Janet joked half truthfully.

Dana giggled. "I felt like Scooby Do, pulling the ghostly disguise off of Bargello."

Even Edna laughed at that.

"So why are we all so sad?" Alice persisted.

"Because we are back to the beginning," Edna replied wearily. "This seemingly haunted quilt shop has no one to run it, and now it's time for Dana to go home."

Dana nodded silently, fingering the brass key that had become her necklace.

Chapter 25

Dana had planned to sleep in. But after tossing all night, she was glad to see the light of dawn clearing the foggy night from the streets. *It is time for Dana to go home*; she kept hearing Edna's words repeated in her head as she tried to sleep.

The group of friends had worked late into the evening cleaning up the seance. Alice collected the left behind coats and scarves; she would take them to the Diner and post a notice on a neighborhood message board where people could pick up their things. Janet offered to take what extra chairs and decorations fit in her truck. "I can use them at my New Year's Eve party. And if not, I'll return them to the tag sale."

Dana looked through the kitchen cupboards of the little upstairs apartment. She wasn't hungry. She'd make some tea and go to the airport; she could find a better breakfast there anyway. There was nothing left to do but pack. When she got to California, she would arrange for an estate sale of the property. She didn't need to—and didn't want to—stay in New England for that.

Dana got dressed and started tidying up. As she made the bed, Dana remembered her first night there, with the Stars quilt and the purple neon light. She would miss this cozy upstairs corner overlooking the street. Or, she could take it with her. Why not pack the quilt? It was hers, after all.

Plus, Angie's gorgeous sweaters, she would take those. Although they would be of little use in California. Then she would pack only a few sweaters. And the quilt books, too. She could learn to make a quilt the way Aunt Angie had. *Careful, you may become addicted to quilting.* The thought surprised Dana, and she stopped in the middle of her chores and sat heavily on the bed. Addicted, like Aunt Angie? No, quilting was Angie's cure. And Dana still needed to find her own...cause.

The bittersweet truth filled Dana's heart. Like pieces aligning, she felt her place alongside Angie's brilliant legacy. The answer to what she owed her heritage was simply gratitude. Dana held the key around her neck with both hands and closed her eyes. *I am thankful for my time here. For the things I've learned, the things I have seen, and the people I have met.*

Then, Dana got up and folded the stars quilt and set it in the middle of the bed. She hadn't given up her promise of looking for the key's lock. But she had run out of places to try.

Ultimately, Dana managed to pick only three sweaters and put them beside the quilt. She went downstairs and got the fishbowl full of notes about neighborhood hauntings, noticing some business cards included. *Hopefully, one will be for a realtor*, she told herself as she dumped the cards on the bed. Smiling to herself, Dana added the satin bathrobe, the one she had worn to meet the quilting class. She added her bathroom toiletries and a tin of Earl Grey from the kitchen.

Standing with her hands on her hips, surveying the pile (which didn't even include the quilting books yet), Dana realized she would need more luggage. And Angie's photo albums, letters, and the music box, she wouldn't forget them. She knew they were all waiting on top of the attic desk.

When Dana slid the pocket door open, the attic was full of sunshine and the essence of the lilac candle. As she ascended the few attic stairs, Dana patted the small quilts stacked inside the framing. Ok, she would also include a few of these in her packing.

The desk was as she left it during the rainy night when she called the winery, before Mrs. McGinty visited with Alana and Bargello. Dana couldn't help chuckling again at the thought of Bargello disguised as a ghost. She should be mad, but it was all too inane. She would write her own cards about the quilt shop, seance and all, and add them to the fishbowl pile. Maybe she would get time to put the cards into a scrapbook. *What else should you do with a ghost?*

And there, at the end of the desk: luggage. Dana had forgotten the attic corner of stored luggage. "Is this whole place a 'Room of Requirements?'" Dana asked, to no one in particular as she began shifting Samsonite and American Tourister. There was even a tweed Hartmann.

When she moved the vintage case, Dana discovered the attic's true hidden secret: a filigree door lock set into the paneled end wall.

Dana shoved the remaining pile of luggage out of the way. She sat on the floor in front of the lock. The brass finish matched the key on her neck. In the morning light, she could identify a horizontal crack in the beadboard that marked the top of a cupboard door. Dana pulled the red velvet roped key over her head and held it to the lock. She looked behind her, and then up at the bright dormer windows over the desk. Part of her was afraid to open the door. What if it was empty? It would top the list of unanswered questions about everything here. But part of her knew it would not be empty. It couldn't be.

Chapter 26

Dana held her breath as she fitted the old brass key into the lock. They slid together easily, and with a bit of extra manipulation, the key finally turned, freeing the latch. As Dana opened the door, morning sun flowed into a yard-long cedar cupboard—a cupboard with three quilts.

Dana's heart leaped into her throat, and she sat briefly with her hands over her mouth. Her eyes filled with tears as she recognized the top quilt as fine, one-inch wide log cabin bars.

Great-Aunt Angie's special quilts! These were the ones she had created in times of crisis. And the lock to the brass key. They were here all along— together. Despite the tears, Dana couldn't help throwing up her arms in victory.

The momentary celebration was unsettled when Dana abruptly realized how close she came to missing this forever. Overwhelmed with emotion, Dana felt like she was on a roller coaster while clearing the luggage from the attic floor. Then she carefully removed the log cabin quilt and spread it over the floorboards.

The quilt was tied with white yarn. The fabrics were random, but the patches were sorted into dark and light sides, just as in the books she had studied. Dana likewise identified the humble red center square of each block. When Dana felt the fabrics, sure enough, the "hearths" were made of silk. *The Professor's ties!* Dana wiped her eyes with her sleeve, wondering what this quilt would have looked like as originally planned; made from insane asylum curtains. Finally, she went back to retrieve the next quilt from the hitherto secret cupboard.

This quilt was folded with the backing out. Dana set it atop the log cabin. Opening the calico, she found gold prongs encircled in orange points, all floating over a blue background stitched with waves. While the log cabin quilt was homey, the Mariner's Compass showed the practiced hand of experience. Dana took the music box from the desk and placed it in the quilt's center. The constellations were identical.

Dana stepped around the sides of the quilt, viewing it from every angle. Finally, she sat in the desk chair, elbows on her knees, watching the quilt. This was a quilt of frustration and sadness, and it showed in the roiling waves stitched around the compass. Professor Stanley had named this quilt as the one Angie made when she learned that her sister had died.

Dana tried to picture her grandmother as a young girl with her older sister. First, Angie was taken away, then their parents, then Angie couldn't find her sister—it all showed in the stitches. Family: a compass over troubled waters.

Dana was ready to view the final quilt in the secret cupboard. She replaced the compass music box on the desk, next to Angie's letters. Turning toward the wall again, Dana realized she was so excited to find the quilts that she hadn't considered the cupboard itself.

This was a purposeful space— a safe inside a semi-secret room. Aunt Angie had built this place for her utmost treasured quilts. This wasn't an attic trunk full of heirlooms that could be spirited away; it was meant to last.

Why so much labor? Was this built from paranoia or assembled through experience? Dana felt she understood. Piece by piece, Angie witnessed her family snatched away and almost lost herself. At least she could protect these few quilts. Maybe Dana wasn't supposed to find this place. Perhaps no one was.

The visible patches of the final quilt were all red, bright in the corner and graduating darker toward the quilt's center. Was this quilt made with joy or sadness? Dana wondered if she would be able to tell which. It was certainly the newest of the three quilts, featuring the utmost artistry. As Dana picked up the last quilt, she could feel the embroidery joining the patches. *Could this be...*

Chapter 27

A *crazy quilt!* Dana's heart raced with certainty. Elated, her hands roamed the small patches of every shape, united by handwork of laces and knots, creating leaves, roses, even a butterfly, and incorporating buttons and beads. But unlike the dark quilts of the book still in her purse, this one sang. The red corner graduated into a purple band angled across the center of the quilt, which turned into black and then midnight blue before finishing in an opposite corner of royal blue. Rather than contrasting stitches as in the book, the embroidery of Angie's quilt matched the color of the patches it joined. The prism ran uninterrupted from corner to corner. It must have taken forever to match all the patches and then plan the stitches. Dana was sure this quilt represented countless months of stitching.

Angie's crazy quilt was the most stunning thing Dana had ever seen. She wanted to swim in the colors. Dana drew the quilt up and wrapped it around her like a cloak. The quilt was extra heavy, and the warmth comforted Dana like a hug across time.

As Dana sank further into the quilt, she realized one of her hands held something different. They both touched backing, but one hand felt satinier than the other. Gently, she set the crazy quilt top down over the compass quilt to have a better look at the reverse. Near one side of the quilt was a large white square sewn onto the backing fabric. In handwriting, the label proclaimed,

My dearest Dana,
I made this quilt for you.
With all my love,
Your Aunt Angela

Dana raced down the stairs. Aunt Angie's Crazy Quilt went in front of her, folded in thirds across both arms.

Looking back, the path made sense, like following a line of stitches.

The attic's cedar cupboard was not a safe—it was a time capsule. If Aunt Angie intended to gift Dana a quilt, she could have listed it in the will and handed it over to an executor, Goerge, Edna, anybody. Instead, she left the key with the letters and the music box. Together, they unveiled the mystery of the Log Cabin and the Mariner's Compass, and they guided Dana on what to search for.

With a free hand, she unlocked the quilt shop door and repeatedly stepped on the industrial light switch, blinking the QUILTS sign on and off as fast as possible. Still carrying the quilt, she ran outside and looked up and down the street. No one there, yet.

Dana could hardly see through her cascading tears. Angie's gift was more than this miraculous quilt, this timeless love, this quilt shop inheritance. It was all these things; it was quilting. The passion that saved Angie was her legacy for Dana.

Dana ran back inside and flashed the sign again. On her fourth trip outside, she at last saw Edna hurrying up the street.

Her Aunt's love instilled a vision in Dana. She didn't know if it would work, and she didn't even care if it would work. Dana only knew that she would do it anyway, no matter what.

"What's happening? What is this quilt! Dana, are you all right?"

Dana took several deep breaths before she could answer. Even then, all she managed to tell was, "Edna, look, I found Aunt Angie's quilts!"

Edna started crying along with Dana.

"Come in, Edna! Call the girls! Come see what I have found!"

They rushed inside and spread the crazy quilt over a central range of bolts. It draped on both sides, showing red on one side, violet on top, and blue on the other side. It was stunning, no matter how you looked at it.

Edna lapped the quilt, unable to decide which beautiful detail to examine first.

"But the sign? Is it broken?"

"I wanted to call my friends, and I knew you must live close by, Edna, since you didn't have a car."

Edna managed to get her phone out, although she couldn't tear herself away from the crazy quilt. Dialing Janet, she asked her to find Margo and hurry to QUILTS. Alice had also seen the QUILTS bat signal and rushed in after parking crookedly in the street.

The friends were together in a moment, proclaiming fascinations over the crazy quilt as Dana told them her story of finally discovering the lock for the old key and Angie's three special quilts.

"Can we see all the quilts?" Janet invited.

"Wait," said Dana. "There is more," and she drew back the side of the draped quilt with the label on it.

The friends cried together as they saw Angie's handwriting and read her simple message to Dana.

"This is why Angie never showed us this quilt," said Edna.

"It was only for you," Alice patted Dana's hand.

"And to think, it never would have been seen if you hadn't found it, Dana." Margo gave them something new to cry about.

"Thank you for showing us your quilt, Dana," Janet acknowledged when she finally could speak.

"There's more I want to share with you all," said Dana, "In addition to more quilts," she clarified in answer to their glances toward the stairs.

Chapter 29

"**I** want you all—to run QUILTS," Dana told her friends.

"We can't afford any down payment," Edna had evidently already thought this through.

"We don't know anything about business," said Margo.

"It is a lovely thought, Dana, but how can we do it?" Alice's voice sounded motherly.

"What kind of shop would you want?" Janet didn't see any possibilities.

"Ladies," Dana stepped between her friends and, with her arms spread wide, drew them together with two on each side of her. "We work well together, and we are creative. The seance showed us that."

"We did work hard last night," said Margo.

"All week long," corrected Dana. "And remember when we first met at quilting class? You managed the class and the walk-in customers just beautifully."

"Well, I see what you mean. Together, we may have the required skills," consented Alice.

"But what kind of shop would it be?" Janet was still skeptical.

"It will remain Aunt Angie's shop," Dana said firmly. "You were all her friends as much as her customers. I've seen that in how you've stood by me this week. You know what she would do. Any business disputes will be settled by asking, 'What would Angie want?' OK?" She looked from one to another. "Plus, plus! Wait for it," Dana held up an index finger, "Aunt Angie left the business plans already set up. There are files with a year's worth of classes and promotions; everything is in place."

"Yes, I see," said Janet. "Like having a running start!"

"That really could work," said Alice.

"But, Dana, how can we afford it?" Edna was always practical. "What would we pay you?"

"Rent," said Dana. "The profits are all yours to reinvest, pay yourselves, or hire help, whatever you need to do. I'll reserve the apartment upstairs. Pay me enough to keep the purple light turned on, and a little I can save for major building repairs whenever needed.

"No doubt, those costs are already on the books. They won't be an added expense for the shop," Margo was getting the idea.

"Dana, that, that is," Edna stammered, for once out of words, her face glowing.

"I think that means yes!" Alice danced into a group hug.

"Yippee!" said Janet.

"Yippee, for sure," echoed Margo.

When the hugging and dancing and crying subsided, Margo asked, "Are you staying here, Dana? Will you live, or work, upstairs?"

"Sometimes," answered Dana with a wink. "Wait until I show you."

Chapter 30

The purple neon light said QUILTS, but the banner over the door read:

GRAND OPENING - THE HAUNTED QUILT SHOP.

Dana was again at the front door receiving guests. This time, she waited on the sidewalk amid pumpkins and a cornucopia of Jelly Rolls. Even though the November day was gray, she had a fabulous sweater to keep warm.

"Come in!" Dana waived to passers-by on the street. "We are showing a special exhibit today," and she handed over a flyer that agreed. "This is the first showing of my Great-Aunt's private quilt collection, newly re-discovered. One of her quilts has never been seen before."

"Oh, excuse me," Dana turned from the newcomers as she saw George arriving in a tweed coat, striding briskly with his cane. "Professor, hi, thanks for coming. We couldn't start without our guest of honor."

George glowed with appreciation. "There is such a good gathering. Angie would be proud. Congratulations, Dana."

"Come inside. I think we have some old friends of yours." Dana opened the door to welcome him further.

"Who?" Professor Stanley couldn't believe the day could hold any more amazement.

"Your ties, Professor," and she led him to the log cabin quilt, now displayed in the first casement window of Angie's shop.

She watched memories wash over his face as he approached the old quilt. He didn't need to tell her. It was all there: the missing ties, Angie working on the quilt, the two of them in the insane asylum, escaping, bound together ever after by that secret. George placed a palm on the quilt and ran his hand over the yarn knots.

"Hi, Professor!" Margo called from the register. She enjoyed doing the figures and had a sweet demeanor that made customers want to return.

Edna waved her hello from the classroom where she was signing up new students.

"Professor Stanley," called Alice, "come see the scrapbook." She loved showing customers the Haunted Album she had created with the fishbowl cards they had collected the night of the seance. Next, Alice would be working on a book to accompany the exhibit.

Janet breezed by with a clipboard. "Let me know when you'd like to see the new fabrics, George. I've set up a special section to showcase them."

"Oh, I'd love to see that," a customer stepped in, overhearing Janet.

"Right this way," Janet left again without actually stopping.

"It's yours if you want it," Dana whispered, indicating the log cabin quilt.

"Aren't you taking these quilts...on a trip?" George was almost too overcome for words.

"Yes, around the country. *Quilt Therapy Exhibit*. For museums and quilt shows, shops just like this one. I'm going to share Aunt Angie's journey with people who are, maybe, seeking a cure." Dana said proudly. "Oh, but not the whole story. Some stormy nights should stay secret."

About the Author

With degrees in history and library science, Ronni Chavez brings a love of research to weaving together her twin passions of writing and quilting. Her debut novel, *The Crazy Quilter*, is a cozy gothic mystery of missing heirloom quilts, a haunted quilt shop, and the healing power of quilting. Ronni says, "Each quilt has a life of its own in memories, relationships, and the joy it provides. As a writer, I'm endlessly fascinated by uncovering those unique tales that unite us in exploring why we create."

In 2007, Road Home Quilting was launched to publish Ronni's quilt patterns. The red and white logo of Road Home Quilting is *Medic*, the block she designed to honor quilting nurses, in companion with the short story, *Aunt Vicki's Quilt*.

When she isn't reading patterns and planning her future UFOs, Mrs. Chavez enjoys swing jazz, oxford commas, dresden blocks, kantha stitches, and everything pumpkin.

Read more at https://RoadHomeQuilting.BigCartel.com.

About the Publisher

Road Home Quilting launched in 2007 with a deep appreciation for quilting's rich history and traditions. We endeavor to share a love of quilting with everyone who enjoys a good story. For readers, *Road Home Quilting* offers cozy quilted stories and poems that explore why we create and celebrate the joy, comfort, and community fostered by the art of quilting. For quilters, *Road Home Quilting* offers patterns that entertain while ensuring your time is well spent and your creativity is rewarded.

Road Home Quilting - **where stories and stitches intertwine.**
Read more at https://payhip.com/RoadHomeQuilting.